# WALKABOUT
# Minibeasts

**Editor:** **Ambreen Husain**
**Design:** **Volume One**

Photographs: Bruce Coleman Ltd.—(J. Markham) 5,
6, (K. Taylor) 6 inset, 22, 23, 24, 29, 31,
(J. Burton) 8, (H. Rivarda) 9, (A. Purcell) 17,
(P. Clement) 26, 27, (F. Greenaway) 30; Frank
Lane Picture Agency—(L. West) 15, (J. Watkins)
18, (G. E. Hyde) 18 inset, 19, 20 inset, (E. & D.
Hosking) 20, 21; NHPA—(N. A. Callow) 4,
(S. Dalton) 11, 12, 14, cover; Oxford Scientific
Films—(M. Leach) 16, (B. E. Watts) 25,
(H. Reinhard/Okapia) 28; Planet Earth Pictures—
(K. Lucas) 7, (S. Hopkin) 13; Barrie Watts—10.

Library of Congress Cataloging-in-Publication Data

Pluckrose, Henry Arthur.
    Minibeasts / by Henry Pluckrose.
        p.   cm. — (Walkabout)
    ISBN 0-516-08119-5
        1. Invertebrates—Juvenile literature.
    2. Animals—Juvenile literature. [1. Invertebrates.]
    I. Title. II. Series: Pluckrose, Henry Arthur.
    Walkabout.
    QL362.4.P58   1994
    592—dc20                                    93-44697
                                                      CIP
                                                       AC

**1994 Childrens Press® Edition**
© 1993 Watts Books, London
1 2 3 4 5 6 7 8 9 0 R 03 02 01 00 99 98 97 96 95 94

# WALKABOUT
# Minibeasts

**Henry Pluckrose**

CHILDRENS PRESS ®

CHICAGO

Next time you walk
down a street or
across a field, look
for the tiny creatures who
share the world with us . . .
the minibeasts.

There are many kinds
of minibeasts.
Some live in large groups
called colonies.
Black garden ants make
their nests in cracks in
paths and sidewalks.
Wood ants build nests
from wood and leaves.

Wasps also live together.
In springtime, the queen
wasp builds a nest.
She chews tiny pieces of
wood until they are soft.
Then she shapes them into
a nest for her wasp family.

Some bees, like the
honeybee, live together.
Other types of bees
live alone.
Bees and wasps have stripes
on their bodies.
This is a warning . . .
"Don't eat me. I sting!"

Not every minibeast
makes a nest.
The woodlouse likes
to live in soil that
is damp.
Look for woodlice
under a brick, a stone,
or a piece of wood.

8

Millipedes also like damp soil. The millipede's body is covered with a hard skin, called a cuticle.
Its body is made of separate parts, called segments.
Each segment has a separate pair of legs.

9

A centipede also has a
segmented body.
It has one pair of legs
on each segment.
It has a hard skin.
Centipedes hunt at night
and feed on worms,
spiders, and slugs.

10

Look closely at the earwig's body.
The joints between the segments
help the earwig move easily.
The earwig protects itself
with its large pincers.

The grasshopper lives in
fields where the grass
is thick.
It has strong back legs and
wings to help it leap from
plant to plant.

Many kinds of minibeasts have wings. The wings of the ladybug are protected by a spotted wing case.

Like all beetles,
the longhorn beetle
opens and spreads
its wing case
when it flies.

This beetle likes to
live in places that are
dry and sandy.
When it hunts, it catches
ants in its strong jaws.
Can you guess why it is
called a tiger beetle?

15

Spiders are hunters.
Some spiders spin a
sticky web of silk.
What kinds of insects do
spiders hunt for food?

16

Some spiders catch their
food in another way.
They hide in the grass
and pounce on any small
creatures that pass by.

17

Butterflies and moths are minibeasts. Many minibeasts have a life cycle like that of the butterfly. The butterfly starts life inside an egg. The female butterfly lays her eggs on leaves.

Later, the eggs hatch
and a caterpillar
crawls out.
The caterpillar feeds
on plants.
It eats and eats and
grows longer
and fatter.

19

When it is fully grown,
the caterpillar spins a web
of silk around itself.
It is now called a pupa.
Inside the pupal case, the
caterpillar changes into
a butterfly!

When it is fully formed,
the butterfly breaks out
of its pupal case.
A new cycle of life has
already begun!

Many minibeasts are insects. Flies are insects. An insect has three parts to its body . . . the head is at the front, the thorax is in the middle, the abdomen is at the back. It has six legs. Like many minibeasts, the fly has two eyes.

There are antennae on
its head for feeling
and tasting the surfaces
on which the fly lands.

Ants, wasps, bees, bugs, moths, and spiders are special kinds of minibeasts. They have no bones. Each has a hard shell on the outside of its body. This shell is a skeleton. It gives the minibeast its shape and protects its soft insides. Human beings keep their skeleton inside their bodies!

Slugs have no skeleton.
They like to live where
it is damp.
A slug leaves a silvery
trail behind it as
it moves.

25

Slugs have no legs.
They move on one
long foot.

The snail moves on one foot—just like the slug. It carries a hard shell. The shell protects the snail from enemies and gives it shelter in bad weather.

An earthworm has
no legs, no feet, and
no skeleton.
Its shape helps it move
easily through the soil.

Some minibeasts feed on plants.
Some minibeasts feed on other minibeasts.
But minibeasts are food too!
Birds eat worms and snails.

29

Frogs eat bugs, flies, and ants.

Some minibeasts, like the fly, carry dirt and disease Some, like the honeybee, give us food. Some are beautiful to look at. And all of them are interesting to watch.

# Index

# About this book

Young children acquire information in a casual, almost random fashion. Indeed, they learn just by being alive! The books in this series complement the way young children learn. Through photographs and a simple text the readers are encouraged to comment on the world around them.

To a young child, the world is new and almost everything in it is interesting. But interest alone is not enough. If a child is to grow intellectually this interest has to be directed and extended. This book uses a well-tried and successful method of achieving this goal. By focusing on a particular topic, it invites the reader first to look and then to question. The words and photographs provide a starting point for discussion.

Children enjoy information books just as much as stories and poetry. For those who are not yet able to read print, this book provides pictures that encourage talk and visual discrimination—a vital part of the learning process.

Henry Pluckrose